GROWING IVY

How to **CRACK THE CODE** on **ELITE COLLEGE ADMISSIONS**

JOHN M. MORGANELLI, JR., M.Ed.

Growing Ivy: How to Crack the Code on Elite College Admissions

 Pensiero Press

Pensiero Press
www.PensieroPress.com

https://Twitter.com/DrCherylLentz
https://www.Facebook.com/Dr.Cheryl.Lentz
https://www.Linkedin.com/in/drcheryllentz/
https://www.Youtube.com/drcheryllentz
https://www.Instagram.com/drcheryllentz/
Email: drcheryllentz@gmail.com

All rights reserved. No part of this book may be reproduced or transmitted in any form or by any means, graphic, electronic or mechanical, including photocopying, recording, taping, Web distribution, or by any informational storage and retrieval system without written permission from the publisher except for the inclusion of brief quotations in a review or scholarly reference.

Books are available through Pensiero Press at special discounts for bulk purchases for the purpose of sales promotion, seminar attendance, or educational purposes. Special volumes can be created for specific purposes and to organizational specifications. Please contact us for further details.

Copyright © 2021 by Pensiero Press

Volume ISBN [TO COME]
Kindle and electronic versions available.

Cover & interior production by Gary A. Rosenberg

Printed in the United States of America

Contents

Foreword vii
Acknowledgments ix
Preface: Learning How to Grow Ivy xi
Chapter 1: Value of an Elite Education 1
Chapter 2: Understanding Application Review 7
Chapter 3: Crafting the College Story 13
Chapter 4: Engaged Volunteerism 19
Chapter 5: What Drives Decisions 27
Chapter 6: Greasing the Squeaky Wheel 35
Chapter 7: Curiosity Is Key 41
Chapter 8: Ensuring Enrollment Diversity 45
Chapter 9: Financial Aid Considerations 51
Chapter 10: Thoughtful College Transfers 57
Chapter 11: Impact of the 2020 Global Pandemic 61
Chapter 12: Achieving Parity in Education 65
Afterword: Remaining Objectively Reflective 73
About the Author 77
Endnotes 79

This book is dedicated to Leon Washington whose leadership both inspired me and helped shape my educational philosophy.

Foreword

As the coach and recruiting coordinator for a prestigious Division 1 school, I fully understand the complexity of the college-admissions process. Studies show that recruitable athletes with good grades and test scores have about a 90% chance of being accepted into the school of their choice. It's about 45% for legacy students. That number of those accepted plummets to less than 9% for well-rounded students who happen to be brilliant. What gives those gifted students the best possible chance to attend an Ivy League or Ivy-like university?

Given these highly competitive stakes, it may not have been all that surprising to learn some wealthy parents illegally paid hundreds of thousands of dollars, even $1.5 million, to get their child or children into a top-tier college or university. They did so knowing that the chances of success in life favor those who have been accepted into one of these schools.

The road to admissions for a highly selective college or university can be very discouraging, but *Growing Ivy* offers a solid blueprint for getting accepted into one of these schools. With years of experience, John Morganelli Jr. understands the challenges of college admissions as well as anyone. In his exceptional book, he examines all aspects of the process—from filling out the application and applying for financial aid—to navigating college life. His insight is invaluable for helping students write powerful essays that capture their strengths and passions, presenting the best possible version of each student to the institution of their choice. John provides helpful examples from former clients and tips on what highly selective universities are looking for.

John breaks down the complexity of college admissions among the nation's top schools in a way everyone can understand. As a college coach, I believe it is not how much we know so much as transferring that knowledge to our young athletes. If they do not understand what you are teaching, then it is of no benefit to them.

This book offers a wellspring of knowledge and is one of the best I have read dealing with the college-admissions process. I guarantee that you will enjoy it as much as I did. John cares about the process and understands the impact of what an excellent education can do for someone. In *Growing Ivy*, he seeks to level the playing field for all of the well-rounded and brilliant students I alluded to who face stiff competition getting into an Ivy League or Ivy-like school, providing them a tremendous opportunity to succeed throughout life.

—Robert Abdullah
Assistant Coach/Recruiting Coordinator,
Men's Track and Field, Princeton University

Acknowledgments

I would like to acknowledge the assistance of Bruce Shutan, a journalist and ghostwriter of 38 years.

PREFACE:
Learning How to Grow Ivy

Ivy is more than a poisonous or climbing plant, "especially one with dark green shiny leaves with five points," according to *Oxford Advanced Learner's Dictionary*. It's also rooted in American culture. Ivy crawls across the quaint concrete and stone buildings that dot the campus of eight prestigious universities officially known since 1954 as the *Ivy League*. The tradition dates back to the late 1800s when several of the schools began planting ivy around their buildings. Legend has it that the Ivy League, which was first used to describe a collegiate sports league, was originally known as the IV League when just four of the eight schools were in existence and, therefore, reflected in those Roman numerals.[1] The term is now synonymous with world-class excellence in higher learning beyond sports, but it transcends academia. Ivy grows extraordinary leagues of managers and entrepreneurs on Wall Street, in Silicon Valley, and elsewhere. This term permeates the personal and professional success of graduates from those elite colleges, as well as Ivy-like institutions to shape their character. The value of this education pays lifelong dividends to those who embark on an uphill climb that's at once difficult and challenging but also transformational and highly rewarding.

GROWING IVY

When I use the term *growing ivy*, I'm describing a process or journey. It's not something that can be done in short order. The seeds of curiosity and a love of learning are sown during impressionable years, culminating in achievements that stretch from school to work. When the students I work with grow their own ivy, so to speak, they're not only preparing for the best possible higher educational experience, but also a purpose-driven life full of knowledge, wonder and accomplishment. When grouped together from all walks of life and socioeconomic backgrounds, they harness creative energy, leverage that brain trust, and breed innovation. Community is the operative word. When working with students, I always inquire about their area of academic interest as it relates to their local community. So if someone is drawn to biology, I may suggest that they contact the local community health bureau to pursue meaningful opportunities related to their interest that will pique the attention of college admissions.

I managed to grow my own ivy while working in higher education—developing a sincere appreciation for this idea when I worked at Cornell. The idea began when I recognized the importance of providing real value to the community that employed me with whom I worked. For example, I would actively seek to resolve the unanswered questions that eluded college-admissions administrators as part of a data-driven approach. This strategy? set me apart from my peers, which contributed greatly to our overall success. While at Lehigh University, one of the nation's top national research universities, I had our institutional research team mine data from the previous 5 years across five different academic tiers from the applicant pool and 13 at Cornell, where the nuances among students were more significant.

There was an academic index that included a combination of Scholastic Aptitude Test (SAT) and Grade Point Average (GPA) scores, as well as indications about whether students toured the campus, came in for an interview or open house, called or went to the website, etc. I then segmented the applicant pool to spot those who were a perfect fit for our school. I also was able to lower the admit admission rate at Lehigh to 26% from 31% and increase the average SAT score to 1326 from 1315 between 2015 and 2016. Doing both in a single year is very difficult to accomplish, but allowed the opportunity to identify a critical component of application review that later in my career enabled me to crack the code on elite college admissions for legions of students.

What's ironic is that I didn't have the benefit of an Ivy League college education. I was a relatively good student who earned strong grades and test scores, but I was still searching for intellectual interests that would fuel my passions and help differentiate me from others. Therefore, I wasn't overly intentional or strategic in my pursuits until my professional career when I began to understand how I could make meaningful contributions and provide value. All the while, education was long seen in our family as an opportunity to grow and live the American dream because neither of my paternal or maternal grandparents were college educated.

My father, who built an impressive legal career and ran for public office, took that vision to heart. It was very much instilled in me when I landed a job at Moravian College, the nation's sixth-oldest institution, where my parents, aunt, and uncle earned undergraduate degrees. My mom and dad lovingly raised their brows when I first started work in college admissions because I was one of those kids whose parents had to gently nudge them to do homework like in so many other families. It may not have seemed so at the time, but this line of work proved to be my calling.

One final note before we closely examine my approach to college admissions. I'd be remiss for not at least addressing the scandal masterminded by William "Rick" Singer that landed several rich and famous parents in jail—fueling a long and salacious news cycle. Harvard, Yale, and Stanford were the only elite schools thus far ensnarled in any schemes associated with the U.S. federal investigation aptly named Varsity Blues. While Harvard University's former fencing coach denied charges that he took at least $1.5 million in payments to secure a place for two sons of a Maryland telecom CEO,[2] Yale's former women's soccer coach pled guilty to accepting nearly $900,000 in bribes to admit students as athletes irrespective of their abilities.[3] Stanford's head sailing coach, one of seven at that school to be approached, pleaded guilty to accepting bribes in exchange for recommending athletic recruits for admission who weren't competitive sailors.[4]

Other prominent universities accused of selling test cheating and fraudulent athletic recruitment include the University of Southern California, Georgetown, Wake Forest University, University of San Diego and University of Texas.[5] While equally shocking and outrageous, these events were an aberration affecting a tiny percentage of the applicant pool. It's extremely rare to find people working at colleges in any capacity who are willing co-conspirators. Nearly all of these individuals value higher education and would never do anything to undermine the integrity of their institution. Between the public humiliation and punishment meted out to those involved, there's no doubt in my mind that wealthy parents and collegiate staffers alike will think twice about participating in surreptitious efforts to admit unqualified students in the future. If anything, the 2020 Global Pandemic will have a more lasting impact on the higher education landscape, but more on that later.

My hope is to share the unique insight I developed to help a wider swath of families get their high schoolers into one of roughly 80 top-tier U.S. universities and proudly watch them reap the lifelong benefits of that experience.

CHAPTER 1:
Value of an Elite Education

To fully understand the power and value of an Ivy League or Ivy-like schools, it's important to appreciate just how rare they are in the pantheon of mainstream higher education. There are approximately 4,000 degree-granting institutions in the U.S, plus an additional 2,200 non-degree granting institutions that include beauty and vocational schools, according to the National Center for Education Statistics (NCES).[6] Degree-granting institutions offer an associate's, bachelor's, master's, doctoral or first-professional designation, while non-degree-granting institutions offer certificates or other formal awards. As earlier referenced, about 80 of those schools are regarded as highly selective, showing up in U.S. News & World Report's annual ranking of the best national research universities and liberal arts colleges.

In stark contrast, there are only eight private universities in the Northeast corridor of the United States that are part of the Ivy League, which include Brown, Columbia, Cornell, Dartmouth, Harvard, Princeton, and the University of Pennsylvania, known in educational circles simply as Penn and Yale. There's also a group called Ivy Plus, which is all the Ivy League schools plus Duke, the Massachusetts Institute of Technology

(MIT) and Stanford. Every 2 years, Ivy Plus deans and directors hold a summit to brainstorm enrollment strategies, and I was fortunate enough to host this event in 2017 in Ithaca, NY, during my time at Cornell. The brain trust they assembled to discuss the landscape of higher education is impressive, but then again, so is the quality of education and overall experience. What makes the Ivy League so extraordinary is the diversity of experience among faculty and administers, many of whom had been at different institutions not only around the country but also worldwide. I found there to be more open-mindedness to new ideas and a deeper level of collaboration. There's a mutual respect among those who are part of these institutions that's palpable and without the structural hierarchy that can stifle creativity. While working for Cornell, I was able to provide value and as well as comfortably and confidently contribute in a meaningful way at the highest levels.

There are a multitude of strategic reasons to pursue an Ivy or Ivy-like education. For starters, students have access to far more resources that make for an increased return on a prudent investment in oneself. While an education at one of these elite schools is obviously more expensive and costs more than $56,000 a year at many Ivies, it's not beyond the reach of lower-income families whose students require significant financial aid or even the middle class.[7] A "need-blind" admissions policy that separates the admissions and financial-aid functions is a merit-based approach that means the Free Application for Federal Student Aid (FAFSA) form isn't actually seen until a student has been admitted. Enormous endowments, donations and grants are used to help finance generous financial aid packages for students. It's also worth noting that the most prestigious schools are so well-funded that 7.75 times more is invested per student than other schools. That translates into an eye-popping $92,000 per student across the Ivies compared with only $12,000 at second-tier institutions.[8]

The fact that these schools are so highly selective and admit only the best and brightest minds results in a higher quality educational experience, which manifests itself in many different ways. Still, there are few U.S. institutions with endowments to fund the cost of education for their enrolled students. The nation's last truly *free* institution of higher learning was the Cooper Union for the Advancement of Science and Art. Founded in 1859, it provided all enrolled students a full tuition scholarship until the 2014 fall semester when this longstanding tradition was no longer economically feasible but then decided in 2018 to reinstate that arrangement.[9] Because most colleges and universities cannot afford to fund education for students, they strategically lower the cost of tuition within the confines of their institutional mission by predetermining the "discount rate" or average percentage the tuition can be lowered on a per student basis. For example, if tuition is $40,000 and the internal predetermined discount rate is 25%, on average students should receive about $10,000 in financial aid ($40,000 x 25% = $10,000). But there are philosophical differences between the purpose and distribution of financial aid dollars from one school to the next.

Although most students may feel discouraged about applying to Ivy League and Ivy-like schools because of the ridiculously stiff competition, all colleges want as many applicants as possible. The reason is simple: the higher number of applications, the lower the acceptance rate, which is a boastful metric that raises their desirability level in the public eye. There are single-digit acceptance rates among the Ivies: Harvard is 4.9%,

Princeton is 5.6%, Columbia is 6.1%, Yale is 6.5%, Brown is 6.9%, Penn is 8.1%, and Dartmouth is 8.8%. The exception is Cornell, my former employer, at 11%.[10] As a partly public and partly private university and youngest of the Ivies founded in 1865, Cornell is rather comfortable with the idea of being the "accessible ivy." Given these daunting numbers, there's never any reason a prospective employer (or anyone else) would need to Google these schools to learn more about the quality of that education. With elite schools, there's always instant name recognition. There's also something to be said about the inspiring atmosphere, nicer amenities, and superior libraries. Inside classrooms, it's commonplace to find award-winning professors featuring Nobel Laureates, distinguished intellectuals, or seasoned scholars.

In addition, there are numerous post-graduate considerations that make choosing Ivies a tremendous lifetime investment. Look no further than a stellar track record of helping graduates rise to higher social and economic strata, with an estimated 70% of students earning middle-class incomes while others build wealth.[11] As recipients of the most robust social capital in academia, they're able to establish meaningful ties with fellow students, academic advisors, speakers at campus events, and members of professional organizations. Access to an illustrious group of alumni represents another invaluable networking avenue considering that the Ivies are a breeding ground for high achievers. Sixteen of 46 U.S. presidents graduated from Ivy League schools, five of whom attended two Ivies apiece.[12] Each of these conduits may help secure lucrative employment opportunities or advance careers later in life, and when the time comes to look for work, Ivy grads have a huge advantage.

Employers have a favorable view of Ivy degrees, which serve

as the ultimate calling card for those who are about to enter the U.S. workforce, run for public office, make their mark in research and innovation or dream of winning a Nobel Prize. Although a degree from the Ivies doesn't guarantee higher income, there's evidence that attendance presents a clear advantage. One study, for example, found that the most successful Ivy League grads are paid 35% more than their top-earning counterparts from other universities.

Others speculated that it could well be that Ivy Leaguers are simply hardworking and career-minded by nature, able to leverage wealth and family connections, or a combination thereof.[13] Whatever the case, graduates of the nation's most elite universities are more easily accepted as an authority in their field, which can help them publish books and articles, as well as raise money for startups in business. The question is, how do students acquire the knowledge necessary to obtain this powerful calling card that others around them will notice the rest of their lives? It starts with understanding how the application-review process works and type of information that needs to be shared to gain admittance.

CHAPTER 2:
Understanding Application Review

After a decade reading tens of thousands of college-admissions applications, I knew it would be daunting to help even qualified students earn offers at highly selective institutions. The students and their families that I help yearn for a simple formula: GPA + SAT = OFFER. But that's not the way it works. The review process is highly subjective, and there are several moving parts to making a compelling argument as to why a student should be admitted to one of the nation's best universities based on their academic performance, involvement with activities in school and across their community, intestinal fortitude and other factors. But I've designed a template for families to follow that anticipates all of these variables and leads to success.

The application review process at most universities looks something like:

1. Applications are sorted or filtered based on institutional review processes (i.e., geographic region, academic program, ethnicity, high school, etc.).

2. First review is often conducted by either a seasonal application reader or regional admission manager.

3. Second review is often conducted by a more experienced admissions officer.

4. After two rounds of review some files are ready for a decision and others require additional discussion by an admissions committee.

College admissions officers interpret things differently and have their own personal priorities. There's quite a lot of turnover in this area. Application readers often change from one year to the next, making it impossible to spot decision patterns. Many admissions readers at highly selective universities are seasonal part-timers who make the initial assessment. At Cornell, for example, I would hire approximately 40 such people every year to help us read applications for 8 to 12 weeks. But having a general understanding of the audience is essential. I feel comfortable saying that a significant percentage of the admissions readers are generally humanities or social science educated liberal females between the ages of 22 and 40 who are apt to listen to National Public Radio, aka NPR. But generalizations only go so far. While some readers might love an applicant's personal statement or supplemental essay, others will not share that enthusiasm. Mindful of this typical reader profile, the point is that even if those words don't exactly resonate with everyone the goal is to submit a quality document that represents the student well.

During the initial review the reader will document pertinent information about a student's academic rigor, extracurricular engagement and will oftentimes make some level of recommendation (i.e., make an offer, reject, defer or waitlist). Once that application is reviewed, it typically will go to a more senior

Understanding Application Review

full-time staff member who serves as a second pair of eyes. If both readers disagree, then the decision can be subject to a full selection committee review, which often happens less than 10% of the time. Most often, the school's director of admissions or dean must sign off before any decision is finalized.

Applications are typically sorted or filtered by standardized test scores. For a majority applicant (white or Asian), the student should be somewhere close to the university's 75th percentile. A simple Google search of "Cornell average SAT score" will reveal four numbers (Critical Reading: 680-750 and Math: 710-790).[14] The two lower numbers are Cornell's 25th percentile SAT scores. Thus, 25% of enrolled students at Cornell scored 1390 and below. Generally, these students are underrepresented minorities, those interested in unique academic programs, VIP candidates with connections to the university and athletes. The two higher numbers are Cornell's 75th percentile. Thus, 50% of the enrolled students scored between 1390 and 1540. And finally, the remaining 25% scored above 1540. My general rule of thumb for majority applicants applying to typical majors is that in the early decision round they should be around the 50th percentile and in the regular-decision round they should be around the 75th percentile (more on this later).

After the applications have been filtered or sorted by standardized tests, most universities will start with the high school transcripts in order to examine a student's curriculum choice (i.e., humanities, social sciences or science, technology, engineering and mathematics classes (STEM) and the degree to which they sought to challenge themselves (i.e., number of Advanced Placement (AP), or International Baccalaureate (IB) courses). To be seriously considered by the top-tier universities students are expected to complete a certain number of advanced courses each year. Generally, to be seriously considered at a highly selective institution students should take at least approximately 8 to 12 advanced courses if offered by the high school. Some students will have taken more than 15 advanced courses throughout high school with one ambitious former client completing 22 of them, including IB courses, in the student's area of academic interest.

After reviewing these baseline academic measures, application readers consider structured in-school extracurricular activities managed by teachers or mentors, which are the lowest hanging fruit of all student involvement outside the classroom. People would be amazed just how many students have almost no footprint in this area. It's a blank canvas for many whip-smart kids, oftentimes through junior year, because they're so academically focused. And if they're also taking private piano lessons or something similar, then there's no time for much else. That's a big red flag for colleges that expect students to take advantage of the resources that are available to everyone. It's also important that in-school extracurricular activity must make sense within the context of what students want to study. It's logical to expect someone who's interested in mathematics to become a Mathlete or get involved in Science Olympiads or a robotics organization.

When it comes to volunteerism opportunities outside the classroom, college admissions officers may believe flying across the country to help poor people, building homes in New Guinea or interning at an influential politician's office has more to do with parental access or wealth than a student's actual interest or passion. What I like to do is craft less structured opportunities in the local community that broaden a student's perspective on areas of academic interest. Built around pure curiosity, they will be seen as more meaningful than ones that were created by privilege. I call these self-directed activities "engaged volunteerism" in their area of academic interest, but more on that a bit later. As long as an application checks all of the right boxes, then it will be much easier to sway virtually anyone that a student belongs on their campus in the fall. But the sum of those parts must portray a consistent message that adds perspective and meaning to the story being told.

CHAPTER 3:
Crafting the College Story

In assessing a student's qualifications for Ivy League or Ivy-like schools, college readers obviously will consider academic rigor, grades and test scores. It also helps when candidates are able to demonstrate that they're hardworking or goal-oriented. But extracurricular engagement is where the best candidates rise to the surface. When examining the college application process as a whole, there are essentially two opportunities for a student's voice to come through. As the title of this chapter suggests, they allow applicants to craft what I like to call their *college story*. One part involves a personal statement that's about 650 words and included in the Common Application that goes to every single college to which an individual applies (I will explain more about the Common Application in the next chapter). In addition, there are generally supplemental essays wherein each college asks applicants to answer very specific questions. While these essays vary greatly from one college to the next, there are usually one or two of them in the 500-word range, though some are half that length and others like Stanford require responses to eight different very short essay prompts.

My larger point is that students often have less than 1,200 words to tell their entire story through a few different writing opportunities. While essays may lay the story's foundation, there are other important components to any application that collectively tell a story, and it's critical that each of those parts complement one another. They include the high school transcript and extracurricular activities, as well as letters of recommendation from a guidance counselor and two teachers with a supplemental source added to the mix, depending on the student's experiences. Since there's no word limit for these letters, they easily can fill two or three pages and represent a solid opportunity to round out an applicant's college story. While there will be personal aspects to share on the admissions application, remember that the story must have an academic focus but also show that someone is well-rounded between their classroom performance and involvement in the world around them evidenced by active engagement.

Once a meaningful academic direction has been identified, I will ask students to ponder what experiences, qualities and characteristics they would want to share that are somehow related to their college story. The next steps are to list all of those elements and talk through all the supporting details. We need to offer concrete evidence that a student is worthy of being admitted to one of the best universities in the country rather than simply provide pontification. One of the things I tell students all the time before they pick recommenders to write letters on their behalf is to have an idea of what the college story will be so that they can complement that narrative. Most guidance counselors and teachers want that direction because they don't know every single student all that well, and have a short period of time to write letters of recommendation.

Many high schools are now asking for *brag sheets*, which offer students an opportunity to tell the counselor or teacher what story they hope to convey in their applications. These materials help supplement college applications. I have found the message that resonates most isn't so much how hard a student works or has overcome obstacles so much as expressing a love of learning. One of the families I worked with wrote what I consider to be a model template for the kind of information that will give their student a competitive edge. The parents of Sam noted that he was educated in China and knew very little English as a seventh grader when they moved to the United States. They credited his natural curiosity and love of learning, along with healthy habits and replaying recorded school courses, for overcoming a language barrier and excelling at an almost endless stream of interests. Sam was described as a world-renowned Rubik's Cube competitor, avid bowler, Kungfu enthusiast and violinist who also enjoyed coding a new video game. Apart from excelling in a number of STEM disciplines, he also was called creative and community focused. "His passion for simply learning about the world around him is unique—and special," Sam's parents wrote.

Whatever shape or form these brag letters take, it's important that a consistent story emerges so that a reader notices the same theme permeating all different aspects of an application from the high school transcript and college essays to extracurricular activities and letters of recommendation. A complementary college story will capture the attention of admissions readers and officers. For example, a student I worked with named Leonard explored his interest in business marketing through entrepreneurship and economics clubs in high school, as well as outside activities involving the Athena Summer Innovation Institute at Barnard and Brown Leadership Institute. In addition, he applied as a social media intern at a local restaurant where he learned "targeted marketing" methods using Facebook and Google platforms. Other experiences included researching whether small businesses make use of technological aids and even offering his local chamber of commerce free training on how its members might leverage user data to better make use of their marketing budget. His impressive presentation was recorded and the link added to his college application file. My larger point is the importance of focusing on academically relevant experiences.

Any inconsistencies will foil this mission. For example, a letter that veers off course from the story that's being told would be a death blow to admission. It's difficult to game the system with elite schools. Since there are fewer students interested in philosophy than computer science, savvy applicants often will declare underserved majors. However, admissions officers are trained to spot any discrepancies with critical eyes that will determine whether such intentions make sense or are sincere based on transcripts, extracurricular involvement and letters of recommendation that have consistent messaging. An example would be a student who applies as someone interested in public health to avoid competition with pre-medical students, but his guidance counselor writes, "John dreams of becoming a physician." Highly selective universities want to know that students challenged themselves in the areas they plan to study there. Thus, if the student's curriculum is mostly STEM-based, it makes no sense to apply as an English major. The next perspective to consider is the application's tone and determining how the college admission reader is going to connect to a student's college story. Given the commonalities among readers and enrollment management admission officers as I noted in the previous chapter, applicants can make educated guesses about the perspective or values of the admissions reader. He or she is likely to highly value social and community structures that emphasizes openness, cooperation, mutual respect, freedom of expression, intellectual humility, and peaceful solutions.

An applicant's job ultimately is to illustrate these qualities through intellectual and/or community based engagement as part of a cohesive and comprehensive college story. I firmly believe the linchpin for distinguishing exceptional applicants from the pack is engaged volunteerism.

CHAPTER 4:
Engaged Volunteerism

There are several ways students can engage in valuable learning outside of the classroom. In-school extracurricular activities, such as clubs and organizations, are considered low-hanging fruit and not overly impressive. This type of participation is necessary because it's expected. There are also extracurricular activities outside of school that could involve, for instance, the Johns Hopkins Center for Talented Youth summer program or a part-time job. A third rail of involvement is engaged volunteerism.

In my first year of college-admissions consulting, I'd have my assistant jot down every single question that was asked of me, then compile and categorize them in an Excel spreadsheet to spot any commonality. It was an eye-opening pursuit. One of the questions that came up over and over again was, what should I be doing for volunteerism? I developed responses and strategies to help students understand a bit better what colleges value. It's definitely not the traditional volunteerism pushed by parents and guidance counselors as part of a high school requirement. Under that approach, most students really have no interest in what they're doing and sometimes a service to the community generally is not overly valued in college admissions. I remember working with one student who presented a list of potential opportunities that included volunteering at a soup kitchen and shadowing at a hospital. While both were worthy pursuits, I suggested she search for something more relevant to her life.

What I do with my students is shift that focus away from *volunteerism* involving some level of service and instead focus on community engagement in an academic area of interest to create real depth in their application. In a largely unstructured environment where students aren't being told what questions to ask or who to speak with and it's not for a competition or project, these activities are perceived as an expression of unbridled enthusiasm for a particular area of interest. Students also are able to show some level of independence and understanding of local community resources. While helping poor families in Nicaragua is laudable, it's important for students to remember they don't necessarily have to travel around the world when there always will be opportunities in their local community to make a meaningful contribution.

There are several students I have worked with whose engaged volunteerism experiences can be emulated by others. One such example is a female who initially wanted to study premed, but given that it's so intensely competitive, I encouraged her to consider the public health route. She ended up reaching out to a local health bureau, and I helped arm her with a list of questions to ask about their mission, intended audience, funding, best practices, community partners and obstacles, as well as resources provided and who determines how they're distributed. Simple conversations with a bureau representative delving into economic, biological, sociological, philosophical and political issues led to almost endless discussions and ultimately a pretty cool internship. But tapping into a harrowing childhood experience gave this student a specific direction that made her pursuit all that more compelling.

While living for a short time in Malaysia at age 10, she became quite ill from lead poisoning in the local water supply. That experience proved to be a defining moment in her life. Here's why: her doctor didn't seem concerned, noting it was a rather common occurrence. His reaction was eye opening for Americans. So I had her research water companies to determine where their water source comes from, how they treat the supply, what condition the pipes are in, and how often they need to be examined. In addition, she examined where lead poisoning come from, how it's fixed, and the difference between drinking water in developed countries vs. undeveloped countries. Her goal was to prevent something like this from happening to other children in underdeveloped countries. The story came together quite nicely because we went through that process of making sure the transcript and extracurriculars supported it. In fact, she decided to do some type of water testing analysis in her high school chemistry club. What we ultimately did was connect a meaningful experience to her area of academic interest, which of course is the chief objective behind engaged volunteerism. A compelling story to illustrate simple curiosity and true intellectualism was built around an ability to ask questions without someone telling her where to go and what to do. There's no doubt that college admissions readers will believe she's interested in this area.

Another student of mine is very interested in music, but his mom wants him to pursue business. So I asked if he had any questions about business and music and thought about combining the two areas. At some point, there's going to be a business question behind it for him. Obviously, he will need to make money. I asked him to find out how many Long Island music businesses were making records, hosting music shows, selling musical instruments, conducting music competitions, and holding online classes. Also up for further examination was how local music businesses marketed themselves to the community, as well as what pricing, discount, and coupon strategies they used to attract customers. Other questions quickly followed about how they track listener engagement, use influencers, whether they offer a free and paid service, how many local music businesses have more than one revenue stream, which revenue streams were most viable in the current environment, and how social media changed and increased the opportunities available to start a music business. In addition, I asked him to research how many local music businesses transitioned to digital media to sell their products and services and built an ecosystem with other local businesses to thrive.

Armed with tons of questions, he called several local music companies to see what products and services they offered, as well as value-added services such as giving away free music, discounted products, coupons, platforms for fan interaction, music competitions, talent shows, etc. By the end of his engaged volunteerism, he created a video on how to start an online music business to cater to Long Island residents and launched it on YouTube based on the information he collected from local music businesses and his research. He also had the option to invite some of the business owners and artists to participate. What eventually happened was that the student became super intrigued because he loves music and was actually able to find answers to these pressing questions. He went from not having a clue as to what he wanted to do to becoming interested in music-business entrepreneurship. And it really started with just a simple question. It's exciting to see that change in direction. I can hear the passion and excitement in their voices when they discover there's something interesting in the world for them. That's a neat moment.

Yet another community engagement plan I crafted was for a student interested in physics who was asked to examine whether his high school or others in New York City incorporated solar power for their energy requirements. As with the others I have worked with, a list of questions were compiled concerning how much of their energy needs were met by solar panels, how it has reduced both greenhouse gas emissions and costs, why solar panels were installed rather than equipment for harnessing other renewable resources for energy, how direct current from solar panels converted is to alternating current, etc. We also explored solar arrays and photovoltaic cells, the solar potential of different areas in New York City, how solar technology is being improved or made more efficient, how students can be educated and prepared for a clean future, and what concepts in physics would be central to this issue. Among the sources made available for researching this project: the Department of Energy (DOE) and the New York Power Authority websites for information about solar arrays, as well as collaboration with other physics students to generate content that could be distribute to the high school student community.

My favorite example involves a student interested in computer science who also happened to be a volunteer firefighter, but it wasn't something he talked about much. We combined those two areas for a unique engagement plan, reaching out to his hometown fire department to learn if they did anything about computer aided design modeling to combat smoke inhalation. He was told no and then put in contact with a local contractor who worked with the department and showed him how casinos use computer science modeling to ensure that air is being properly ventilated. The contractor also shared how buildings are now being built to be more fire resistant.

Another area of exploration that intrigued this young man was the impact computer-aided dispatch was having on emergency phone calls. The student reached out to the New York State 9-1-1 coordinator and had a two-hour-long conversation with her. He learned that there's a suite of products from companies like Hexagon, which New York City used, as well as Tyler Technologies and Motorola. A neighboring county used another resource. This research gave him a sense of what that process was like when a 9-1-1 call is made, which led to investigating what type of equipment other nearby counties were also using and accessing databases to share information. He learned that New York City is eyeing a next-generation 9-1-1 system in the next few years with enhanced features that support GPS location for wireless phones. While the location of landline calls can be immediately pinpointed, wireless phone call signals are triangulated to towers, resulting in a less specific area. After compiling lots of valuable information, he reached out to some of these tech companies to learn more about the cost and quality of their products, as well as the availability of different packages and new features. The end game on his project is to present recommendations for improving 9-1-1 emergency dispatch services to local city council meetings that open the floor for public comments. His appearances were videotaped and added to his college-admissions application. I also asked him to write an op-ed piece about this topic for a local newspaper, with a link to the article that that could also be added to his admissions file.

Engaged Volunteerism

College admissions readers pore through thousands of applications with only about 15 minutes to read each one. They generally look for consistent messaging, and the more memorable the application, the more likely a student will be admitted. Layering in what other people have to say about an applicant will either enhance or distract from the story that's being told. While academic competition, computer coding and similar feats are still needed, most students who apply to highly selective schools already have all of that under their belts. Engaged volunteerism in the local community is the next level, and quite possibly, the ultimate vehicle for differentiation. These activities show a willingness to think about how a student's skillset could benefit the people around them, and that's important as well.

Many students don't ever reach this exceptional level of volunteerism, but those who do usually get into good schools. Which brings me to a larger point I think is worth articulating: Older people often dismiss this next generation as lazy or entitled. But as someone who has worked closely with these kids on a daily basis, I strongly disagree. Some of them are brilliant, socially conscious and excited. Even in the face of a frightening worldwide pandemic, the human race is generally getting better. We're learning, growing and evolving, and I see that in these kids, which leads me to believe the future is incredibly bright. Engaged volunteerism clearly can shine as the centerpiece of a college-admissions application, which obviously lays the groundwork for a series of critical decisions that will establish a reasonable timetable and expectation for how this process will unfold in a high school student's senior year.

CHAPTER 5:
What Drives Decisions

The number of college-admissions applications are rising because students are applying to more schools in the face of growing competition, and as such, higher demand for academic excellence. Thanks to the Common Application (Common App), which came to fruition in the 1970s, students can fill out all of their pertinent information just one time and send the application to as many colleges as they want. It continues to fuel the trend toward multiple college applications, an idea born when 15 forward-thinking colleges and universities sought to simplify the college-admissions process. The Common App, which is now a nonprofit membership organization representing nearly 900 diverse institutions of higher education in all 50 U.S. states and 20 countries, has benefited educational institutions in a substantive way.[15] The Common Application keeps nearly $5 per application and the college keeps the rest. At Cornell, the application fee is $105. Multiply 50,000 applications by $100, for example, and the ensuing $5 million quickly adds up—padding a college's coffers.

Making it much easier to apply has, no doubt, ratcheted up the competition to a point where students are now applying to as many as 15 schools. That's two to three times what it used to be over the past few decades. This makes it increasingly difficult to focus on one or two destinations anymore. The prevailing thinking is to bundle groups of about five schools as a reach, target and safety. In nearly all cases, Ivy League or Ivy-like schools will be a reach, even for valedictorians with a 1550 SAT score and terrific grades who still will need to differentiate themselves through outstanding community involvement or the way they view the world. When you have admit rates in the single digits and focus on a specific cohort (i.e., students interested in STEM areas from New York), it's perfectly reasonable to expect that fewer than 5% of applicants will be accepted. A cohort is any grouping of students that colleges and universities consider valuable such as ethnicity, an academic program, high school, standardized test, etc., for apples-to-apples comparisons. While an Ivy-Plus institution like Duke University may seem like a target for students who are in the top 10% of their high school class with teachers and parents alike believing they're brilliant, it's unrealistic to call it a *target* unless they're *hooked* into the school in some way. This is an informal term that nearly every college uses to describe various ways that students can hook themselves into a university. Those hooks turn certain students into an institutional priority to, for example, increase diversity or the number of students in underserved academic programs. Two common hooks involve star athletes, whose performances please booster clubs and alumni who help pad endowments, and a so-called legacy candidate whose family members have attended. Another hook could involve females in STEM majors, which was the case when I worked at Cornell.

Applying to colleges can be a long and arduous process for students and school administrators alike, but there's a clear strategy that can be employed to everyone's benefit. Universities created the early decision (ED) option, known in higher education as ED for short, to raise their desirability by being more selective. It's now commonplace for more than half of college enrollment attributed to early acceptance. This means a college needs significantly fewer offers of admissions to pin down their incoming class, which keeps lowering their admit rate and offers a deeper sense of security. Students who apply by about November 15th vs. January 1 of their senior year for regular decisions, or RD for short, and earn an early green light commit in writing to enroll in that particular school. Applying early decision gives them an advantage.

It's worth noting that colleges oftentimes are more willing to accept weaker candidates in early decision because a commitment has been made, it lowers the admit rate and builds the next class. Underrepresented minorities, low socioeconomic candidates and students who don't typically leave geographic regions generally aren't in the early decision applicant pool, which is dominated by white and Asian students from more affluent homes. That means colleges have to fill out the rest of their class with other institutional priorities during the RD round, and most White and Asian applicants who didn't apply ED are probably not getting in because space will be limited. Harvard, Princeton, and Yale don't have early decision because they don't need to; their yield rates are second to none, whereas Columbia, Cornell, Penn, and Stanford do offer that option. Some elite schools such as New York University (NYU), the University of Chicago, Lehigh, and Vanderbilt took the concept to a higher strategic level. The thinking was that while their ED applicant pool was solid, offering a second round of early decisions could yield ED applicants who didn't get into Ivy League or Ivy-like schools and therefore, could strengthen their incoming class. The applicant pool for ED Round 2 is generally much smaller than the first ED round and those students don't learn whether they've been accepted until early to mid-February, whereas the RD applicants will not find out until mid-March.

Given all of these options for deciding when to apply for college, how do students build a list of schools they want to attend? I always suggest starting with the ED Round 2 option, which most of the students I work with don't even know exists. This strategy is low-hanging fruit because it establishes a solid second choice early on in the application process. If a student wants to put NYU on that list, I closely examine his or her academic ability and determine the likelihood of an early acceptance by associating the school's admit rate with someone's grade. I also mine demographic data. An Asian student living in a high-export state, for example, generally needs to be in the 75th percentile of standardized testing rates, which would be about 720 for reading and writing and 790 for math at NYU, totaling 1510. If the student has a good shot at getting into selective schools, then I can be more aggressive in our first choice for ED. Thus, determining the likelihood of getting an offer of admission helps inform our ED Rounds 1 and 2 conversation in addition to helping build the RD list of schools.

To gain a better understanding of how various timetables affect admissions, let's examine some of the key differences and nuances associated with these processes. RD and early action (EA), which is an opportunity to apply early, are generally non-committed application rounds. The clear advantage of EA is quickly finding out about an early acceptance and feeling good about having somewhere to go, even if the applicant decides not to attend. Waiting for other offers allow students to compare financial aid packages. It's worth noting that a university does not have the same level of investment in an applicant that doesn't commit to attending in the fall. In some instances, it actually may be harder to get in EA. That's because a university is trying to determine whether students who applied early are better or more unique than the crop who are more likely to come in RD. If EA applicants are considered part of a superior group, then the school would hope they choose them before hearing back early from others. It's reasonable to assume that the cream of the EA crop may decide to apply multiple elite schools. If, on the other hand, EA applicants are deemed similar to others who typically apply, then those students are deferred into RD and compared to everyone else. This leaves them at a clear disadvantage because students who wait for RD have an opportunity to work on their application for an extra month and a half. The nation's most highly selective schools have started to employ something called *restrictive* EA, which is almost a hybrid between ED and EA whereby students can only apply to one school. This approach is essentially a response to high school guidance counselors griping that it's unfair to make students commit to an institution so early in their senior year. But they have the upper hand because whoever gets into Harvard, Stanford or similar schools never wait. In contrast, RD is just a very technical application process with the latest of all deadlines. All applicants are being compared to the masses and are not committed to attending. Rather, they may compare all of their offers and financial aid packages. Every college and university provides an opportunity for RD students to wait until May 1 of their senior year to actually decide whether or not they are enrolling and make a deposit.

One wildcard to consider in the college-application process is a student's chance of getting off waiting lists, which I will explore a bit further in the next chapter. When I was at Lehigh and Cornell, we could have re-filled the entire class a second time just through the waitlist. My first year at Lehigh, we took just nine kids off the waitlist from a pool of 4,000 applicants. So understanding how the college uses a waitlist and the chance of getting off of it is important just to know whether those are viable options. All that data is available online, but it is important to understand how to interpret the information.

For applicants who aren't hooked, which involves most of the applicant pool, as well as those for whom early decisions or waiting lists aren't an issue, initial discussion may center around determining what school is the right fit. This issue can help steer decisions made by some students and their families. It's the college-admissions equivalent of an undeclared major. Knowing where to apply is a process that may be fraught with uncertainty. Where admissibility is concerned, I will weigh a student's transcript and their 75th percentile SAT scores at the college. Academics drive that conversation. But many discussions are over social experiences. Fraternities and football, to some degree, are a cultural phenomenon. Tons of people often tailgate at a college football game who don't even like the sport. They're just there to hang out and have fun. Remove that from the equation and a certain aspect of the experience radically changes. For some students, it's important to find the right fit. Interestingly enough, I have found this to be the case with white students and their families. But for others, such as my some of my Asian and Indian clientele, the focus is on a university's name recognition more than location and size. I always ask my students to think carefully about what they value in educational experiences. Is it small class size and one-on-one engagement with faculty or are they okay with a teacher's assistant instructing 250 students in a seminar? Is it a social or cultural component? Do they prefer a competitive or collaborative academic culture? Once academic credentials are layered over the top of that, it quickly pares down their list of priorities. Any discussion around finding the right fit also typically considers educational expenses, which nowadays is becoming an increasingly important consideration as I'll examine in more detail later on.

The bottom line is that there are several tangible steps students can take to get noticed, improve their college-admissions strategy and be admitted into one of the nation's most coveted institutions of higher learning.

CHAPTER 6:
Greasing the Squeaky Wheel

Applying to selective colleges requires real effort, and once the work is done, it becomes a waiting game—literally and figuratively—given all the stiff competition students face. There are two general types of college waiting lists: traditional and progressive. Under the former approach, schools attempt a perfect enrollment. One example is the enrollment target is 1,000 and the historical yield is 25%. The admissions director will likely make 4,000 offers of admission to enroll the 1,000-student class. Under the latter approach, schools purposely under enroll a class. That means at the same school the admissions director may only admit 3,500 students in an effort to purposely under enroll so as to strategically use the waiting list to enroll the final 125 students (500 fewer offers x 25% yield = 125 fewer students). Strategically using the waiting list in this fashion has multiple benefits. First, it will lower the school's acceptance rate. Most universities will actually call waitlisted students *before* offering them admission to determine their interest. If the student no longer appears interested, the admission officer will likely not send an offer of admission. If the student demonstrates significant interest, then the admission officer will likely send an offer of admission. Thus, the yield on the students taken off the waiting list is very high (often over 80%. I used to jokingly refer to this practice as Early Decision 3 because of the propensity for very high yield rates). To get off the dreaded waiting list and alleviate any anxiety that has mounted during that all-important senior year, the proverbial squeaky wheel often gets the grease. But it's a delicate balancing act. For example, students who send two appropriately timed emails during April may be more apt to catch the attention of an admissions counselor and improve their chance of being admitted, whereas those who excessively contact the school or do nothing may be seen as an annoyance or never move off the list. In short, they need to be proactive and reach out.

Here's why: College admissions officers are human and can be persuaded. After reading countless applications and *yielding* students from September through May, they're exhausted by May and frankly thinking about summer vacation. When it comes time to tap the wait list as part of an enrollment strategy, they're going to choose those who have shown interest by emailing, calling or visiting the school. Even though colleges implore applicants not to show up, I've seen cases where eager students show up with their parents and are accepted on the spot. By spring, the balance of power in college admissions at even some of the best schools has suddenly flipped from colleges deciding who's getting in to students deciding whether to pursue the institution. At that point, colleges return to recruiting mode to round out their admissions work for the upcoming school year, and depending on the school, there's an opportunity for negotiation. One scenario, for instance, might involve appealing an earlier decision not to provide financial aid or a merit scholarship.

There also are lessons for colleges that can be gleaned from waitlists. In their haste to turn out the lights for summer, some school administrators may be in store for a rough landing as the school year winds to a close. Case in point: Bucknell University, a fabulous school dropped its essay requirement to lure more students from different demographic groups. Applications went up significantly because applying was less work, but the problem was some of those students were less interested and simply applied because it was easy. The result was a lower than anticipated yield and a long summer of managing waiting list calls. The cautionary tale for other schools is that they must be extremely careful from an enrollment perspective about what's done to the application and how it can affect their applicant pool.

The annual rite of spring involving waitlists is just one of several segments in the college-admissions season. What's most important is that families stay engaged throughout the year. I employ with all of my students a Six-Touch Plan that was part of the recruitment strategy when I was at Moravian College. As admissions officer, my job was to get each student to "touch" the school in half a dozen different ways. For example, if someone were interested in theology I'd connect them with a religious group leader at the school, while those who wanted to major in economics would be referred to an appropriate faculty member. I'd also connect applicants who were interested in research with students who had experience in that area. Our thinking was that it took six different contacts with the institution for applicants to develop a meaningful understanding of the school culture and what it has to offer.

A female student I worked with named Amanda who was interested in engineering and attending Lehigh University where I used to work was very effective at implementing my

Six-Touch Plan. While soccer was hugely important to her in high school and she was captain of her team, she didn't plan on playing the sport in college, but since athletics were important to her, I suggested that she reach out to Lehigh's intramural coordinator. She wanted to get a sense of how club sports would differ from intermural sports. Amanda also reached out to the assistant soccer coach just to see if they ever take walk-ons. Another area of interest was 3-D printing, which she had done in high school using a 3-D printer her parents had purchased for her. Having an inside track at Lehigh, I knew they had a huge 3-D printing and suggested she reach out to the person who's in charge of the printing lab who I remembered was very friendly. They spent about 90 minutes looking at what Amanda had created and how that could have worked differently in their lab, which turned out to be a powerful experience. Many kids don't ever get this specific when they visit schools, so that was a big plus for Amanda. As someone who also was really engaged in volunteerism, she contacted the president of an organization that helped Lehigh students become engaged in the local community. Another invaluable contact she made with the help of the 3-D lab administrator was with an engineering faculty member with whom she discussed the different disciplines in engineering because she wasn't completely sure which direction to pursue. High schoolers often times know about electrical and mechanical engineering, but they may not be as familiar with industrial engineering. So Amanda was able to gain meaningful insight into the intro-level engineering class projects that would cover all of the different steps of engineering available at the school.

With the benefit of having contacted these five individuals (it may not always be possible for all six recommended introductions to be made), it felt like she really understood the institution. The process improved her application because she knew what was available, was available to assess the school culture and get a feel for what it's like to be a student there—all of which she was able to write about. Perhaps even more importantly, she actually knew that this was a place that she really wanted to be. Lehigh was not initially her first choice, and she didn't apply early decision. But because of the way Amanda investigated through a variety of different people, she really became interested and comfortable with the idea of attending Lehigh, whose graduates had the nation's sixth-highest highest salary. This greatly intrigued her. The Six-Touch Plan reduced her overall anxiety about the college-application process as she began to recognize there are some amazing institutions outside of the Ivy League.

Although there are key differences from one elite school to the next, there's a universal truth involving students who want to distinguish themselves in some way through any of those touches. It's all about making a good impression. For example, the way applicants present themselves while on a campus tour, at a college fair or interview may be just as important as the content of what they have to say. A story from earlier in my college-admissions career may serve as a teachable moment. Asked to represent Moravian at an important deans and directors night involving colleges in the Lehigh Valley, I donned the only suit in my wardrobe with a red and black power tie. Everyone at the event was significantly older, which made me feel a bit insecure. But to overcome any discomfort, I introduced myself to every single dean and director, firmly shook their hand, sat down and gave a relatively thorough report with plenty of data to support my talking points about the challenges we faced. I caught the attention of a gentleman by the name of Leon Washington at Lehigh University who was one of the few admissions people I've met who wore a suit to work every single day. He immediately noticed my suit and tie, the latter a replica of one he had in his own wardrobe. He also liked that I came prepared. "Rarely do people come so well-prepared with data," Leon later said after he recruited me for Lehigh. "Anyone can show up and pontificate, but you rattled off real data, and I was impressed." Leon always has notes. Then he goes, "I leaned over to Chris Hooker-Haring," who was Vice President of Enrollment at Muhlenberg College at that time, and said, "That guy's going to work for me." Not 6 months later, it actually happened.

Universities are as complex as humans. They're dynamic and every subdivision within the organization to some degree can be somewhat unique. While six points of contact can be time consuming, I recommend students have at least three interactions involving administration, faculty and students to get a strong sense of what the university values through the different programs it offers. With the 2020 Global Pandemic shutting down traditional fall travel, college fairs and school visits, the pandemic actually heightened the need for a Six-Touch Plan. There are plenty of online programs, academic fairs or student networking opportunities that applicants can tap into and some institutions are literally counting how many times they engage. The more interaction, the better someone's chance of getting into their top choice. But it cannot be forced down a student's throat. There has to be real interest or sincerity, if not unbridled passion. Perhaps the biggest asset of all is simple curiosity.

CHAPTER 7:
Curiosity Is Key

If the beloved monkey known as Curious George ever applied to the Ivies in one of his cartoon episodes on television, he'd more than likely get in. It may seem like a silly analogy, but I think curiosity is a fundamental difference between students who consider education a means to an end and those who view it as a tool that helps them create something new. The ones who get into top-tier schools are consuming information at a voracious pace not just because they love it, but also because they believe it's putting them one step closer to providing their own original contribution to whatever they're interested in pursuing. Curiosity is a driving force more so than earning a specific grade or winning a competition, and there is power in numbers.

When you place a large group of truly curious people into the same environment, amazing things happen. Curious people posing interesting questions to one another breeds creativity and innovation. And so, I think the collegiate experience is not necessarily based on classroom learning or what job will be landed after graduation, but rather engagement and communication with like-minded, curious and passionate people. There's increased value to that not just in the daily college experience, but also the way an individual views the world. With individuals who are really excited about what's going on around them, nothing seems impossible, and having access to this network of impressive thinkers for the rest of your life is really powerful. Ten or 15 years post-college, I think that experience only intensifies the intellectual and professional journeys because of the mark elite college grads have made on the world.

Developing this mindset isn't easy. The number-one problem with students I help is they're unsure what they want to study or pursue as a career. I always encourage them to put forth some time and energy into discovering what they find intriguing in the world—and be patient. Explorers don't always find what they're looking for right away; it's an active process. The underlining goal is to have them think about making an original contribution to the world, and it doesn't have to be some type of invention. It can simply be something that they're excited to spend energy on to improve the lives of people around them.

I also ask my students to learn about what's going on in the world. One suggestion is to download the National Public Radio (NPR) App, click on things they find interesting and listen for 30 minutes. For students who are interested in business, I suggest an excellent podcast called Business Wars. I remember what it was like at their age and how frustrating it is to be so uncertain about your path in life. My parents used to tell me to read the newspaper when I was young. I never did. Ever. I found it very boring. Today I can see that what's going on in the world now is actually more intriguing than the fictional plots on television. I encourage and challenge my clients to be conscious of what is going on in the world around us. Because every day is a new discovery or new crisis. Some students are significantly more engaged these days than maybe I was at their age, but many still need encouragement. When they don't know what's going on in the world it makes it difficult to start exploring. Simply informing oneself through something as simple as 30 minutes of NPR is a terrific jumping off point to independent, community-based exploration.

A few of the students I worked with were able to channel their curiosity in ways that serve as a template for involvement in meaningful activities that will get them noticed at elite schools. One such example involves a high school senior who wants to be a sociologist and is very concerned about homelessness, which has since been exacerbated by the Global Pandemic's impact on the economy. I sent him an article on NPR about the eviction crisis in America, which really intrigued him. So he decided to converse with homeless people in his area, as well as local county officials about universal basic income and affordable housing initiatives. His research shows an ability to not only ask questions and explore for himself, but also recognize various synergies across different areas of a complex national issue.

Another example involves a student who started his own company selling electronic pieces. He spent an inordinate amount of time on Reddit—a social news aggregation, web content rating and discussion website—building relationships with physicists that actually led to real engineering projects. The irony is that these efforts probably compromised his grades (he had 70s across his entire transcript), but they made a huge impact. He was still admitted to one of the nation's top-five engineering schools. While college wasn't something he was initially considering due to his success engineering computer hardware, but the student changed course—concluding that being in a collegiate environment where people are constantly learning would enable him to fully achieve his vision. But it was almost an afterthought because he was already seeding his own educational experience.

Tying these endeavors to an appreciation for the value of an Ivy League or Ivy-like education lays the foundation for life after college. Building networks with like-minded peers at elite institutions who are young, curious and motivated will dictate at least any initial success and offer a lifetime of value. Such high-quality credentials and network contacts open doors to job opportunities or startup ventures more easily and significantly expands one's worldview. Although there aren't many elite universities across the United States, the good news is that there are as many as 350 schools that could give most students almost everything they could possibly want from a college experience. That involves not only coursework and faculty engagement, but also extracurricular activities and even job opportunities. In this way, our educational system is quite different than kind of the rest of the world. Students who are accepted to highly selective schools don't attend because biology is being taught differently there; rather, it's about the campus environment and experiences. And if they're naturally curious or encouraged to be that way, then it will help punch their ticket to the Ivies. When groups of like-minded young people who are not only curious and academically exceptional are joined together as part of a diverse student body, the environment they enter becomes fertile ground for both creative and innovative thinking. The question then becomes how do highly selective schools ensure that diversity will be part of their enrollment strategy and minority applicants can breathe easier through this process?

CHAPTER 8:
Ensuring Enrollment Diversity

As recent times have shown, the value of diversity, inclusion, and equity has soared across American society. However, affirmative action also has been under fire. We've reached a reckoning on race, while at the same time an increasing divisiveness between liberal and conservative perspectives on social issues that surely will spill over into academia. Colleges pull various enrollment levers that affect their admit rate, but there are no such methods when it comes to diversity. Why so? There just are not enough applicants from underrepresented backgrounds to fill an incoming class in a way that is relatively representative of the community that we live in. It's really about recruitment. There are very traditional ways to recruit, with the most typical for colleges involving fall travel. Schools assign their admissions counselors geographic regions where they travel and get to know high schools and guidance counselors, as well as meet with students. There also are college fairs, which typically happen at night, while sometimes they involve multiple schools. This is boots-on-the-ground marketing. But there's another means of helping move the needle on diversity that serves as an alternative strategy.

When I worked at Lehigh, I heard for the first time about

community-based organizations (CBOs), which generally serve students who are underrepresented and socioeconomically at a disadvantage. We had just started reaching out to these organizations. So we put together a plan to build a database of at least 100 CBOs in different markets throughout the country that would be added to our fall travel. Instead of just going to high schools and college fairs, our counselors also were visiting CBOs and grading the quality of the interaction with each organization so as to determine how much future energy to allocate. At the same time, we also invited CBO leaders, along with high school guidance counselors, to our campus hoping they would recommend Lehigh to a group of students to whom we never really had much access.

CBOs stand in stark contrast to so-called feeder high schools that send quite a few applicants to colleges and universities dependent upon tuition. These are oftentimes more affluent schools in higher-income areas, which is where many colleges spend much of their time. Given this practice, engaging CBOs in a more meaningful way made sense to me. We even added into our application a question about whether the applicant is working or has ever worked with a CBO so that we could start capturing this type of data. These efforts doubled our diversity numbers in terms of drawing more under-represented applicants during my tenure, and I decided to employ the same strategy when I arriving at Cornell.

What we found was that CBOs were typically designed to be an after-school support system for students where they could do homework or be tutored. While there were some White and Asian students in the mix, many were Black or Hispanic, which were the groups we were attempting to recruit. But the common denominator was that they all hail from lower-income families. So when visiting one of these organizations, I'd share a short PowerPoint presentation with an overview of how to apply for financial aid. This information is invaluable because schools that are need-blind make decisions without knowing any details about a family's ability to pay. The upshot is there will be no discrimination against underprivileged people.

The first data point that most guidance counselors and independent counselors will consider when determining the affordability of a college education is to whether the institution a student is applying to is *need blind* or *need aware*. The former, as previously explained, is a practice whereby an admissions decision is made without knowing whether the student can afford to enroll. The latter actually considers whether or not families can afford to enroll their student. These counselors overwhelmingly prefer the need-blind approach to help students from low-income families gain admission. But the problem is that it may not be in the best interest of families struggling to make ends meet.

It's, of course, exacerbated by the fact that most students and families don't actually know what that cost will be until very late in the process. To determine whether—and how much—a family may be eligible for in financial aid, several data points must be considered. These include the percentages of students who receive financial aid, overall demonstrated need met and whose need was met 100%, as well as the average grant total. The thinking of financially needy students and their families in the $40,000 annual income range is that if they apply to a need-blind institution that also exhibits above average data points for each of the aforementioned factors, the following scenario will unfold. By the time the school realizes this student's financial standing, he or she already will have likely gained admission and received a strong financial aid package based on those statistics. While need-aware admission no doubt discriminates against some lower-income families, it may allow institutions to be better prepared to fund admission offers for financially challenged students. From an institutional perspective, this practice likely will increase yield and selectivity.

Another problem that arises is some groups face a steep uphill climb within the larger context of colleges attempting to enroll a more diverse student body. While Asians, for example, are obviously a minority in the United States, they are not under-represented in university applicant pools, which means they are often not an institutional priority like Black, Hispanic, or Native American students. There's an inherent disadvantage for Asian students who tend to be very STEM-oriented and interested in computer science. I noticed that competition among Asian students from New York applying to Cornell was through the roof. It comes as no surprise to Asian Americans as well as those of us in the college-admissions space who have followed a six-year court battle over this very issue at Harvard University. As autumn approached in 2020, a federal appeals court agreed to hear arguments challenging college affirmative action policies. The lawsuit, initiated on behalf of Asian Americans, sought to overturn a 2019 U.S. district court decision that found no unlawful discrimination at Harvard.[16]

It was joined by the U.S. Department of Justice, which in August 2020 first publicly accused Ivy League rival Yale University of also discriminating against Asian-American applicants, ordering an end to the consideration of race. A 2016 complaint against Yale, Brown, and Dartmouth that triggered a U.S. Justice Department investigation resulting in a lawsuit filed in federal court in October 2020. Yale is accused of discriminating against Asian-American and White students "based on race and national origin in its undergraduate admissions process, and that race is the determinative factor in hundreds of admissions decisions each year." Yale said its practices comply with a decades-old U.S. Supreme Court ruling allowing race to be considered in college-admissions decisions as long as it's narrowly applied to promote diversity and limited in time.[17]

These developments likely will set the stage for a showdown at the U.S. Supreme Court, which in 1978 narrowly approved affirmative action to promote campus diversity. With the death of U.S. Supreme Court Justice Ruth Bader Ginsburg and appointment of Amy Coney Barrett as her replacement, decades of affirmative action could come to an end. Adding fuel to that legal stance was a 2019 study by the National Bureau of Economic Research that examined the role of wealth, race and access in elite college admissions at Harvard. The findings were eye-opening. For example, while as many as 43% of White students admitted included recruited athletes, legacy students, and others with hooks to the school, it was less than 16% for Black, Latino, and Asian-American students.[18]

Clearly, the United States is at a precipice in the longstanding battle over equal access to higher education. Once students are safely back on campus in a post-pandemic environment with some semblance of normalcy restored, I think we're going to see a very vocal activism over these issues. There will be plenty of angst and unrest on campuses in the beginning once colleges reach critical mass of minority students whose collective voices will only grow louder. Of course, many people will resist any change to the status quo. Not everyone's all on board for change. There will be some clashing of opposing viewpoints on campus. As it relates to college admissions, I don't know how this movement will affect the way applications are being reviewed. Highly selective colleges and universities just aren't down in inner city schools recruiting students, though that's likely to change. If anything, there would be more community-based engagement from those schools. In all honesty, I don't think our educational equity problem is at the college-admissions level. It's rooted at the primary educational level where many young students in lower-income areas start off with fewer resources—an issue I will detail in the final chapter. This leaves them at a terrible disadvantage, and they will spend their early years either catching up or completely losing their way. What's clear is that efforts to ensure more diverse college enrollment are tied to financial aid.

CHAPTER 9:
Financial Aid Considerations

Financial disasters triggered by the Great Recession from the end of 2007 to middle of 2009 and the impact of the Global Pandemic in 2020 were devastating to students and their families. But they also affect academic institutions. What's important to realize is that many schools are tuition-driven, which means they don't rely on endowment, and the cost of higher education will rise to make up for difficult times. Ivies are literally and figuratively in a league of their own and can easily function just off their endowment if they chose to do so. Case in point: Harvard's endowment exceeded $40 billion at the end of the 2019 fiscal year.[19] But the fact is that many schools are 80% to 90% tuition-driven with their endowment matching 10% to 20% of their operational costs.

Generally, colleges are focused on their enrollment total. If a school is aiming for a class of 400, but only 300 have enrolled so far, then it will pull out all the stops to lure in another 100 kids to reach that headcount. That means discounting prices to match the enrollment number by making available more need-based grant money and merit scholarships so that classrooms are filled to capacity. Schools that are tuition-driven are like car salesmen to some degree. "What does it take to get you in this seat today?" is essentially what those pitches boil down to in the waning months of a school year when enrollments are off the mark. The problem with this, of course, is that giving away too many grants and merit scholarships will set an expectation that the school will be discounting at that rate in the future, and sometimes that's not sustainable.

Complicating matters is that students and their families aren't sure about the value of pandemic-triggered online experiences. While vaccinations will drive a return to normalcy, other outbreaks could always cloud the future. People are still going to attend Harvard because the value of that degree, not just the experience. But students are going to be weary of paying the same cost at a small liberal arts college that is less selective, especially if it's private. So what those schools will need to do is discount their tuition. If that happens, then they must figure out how to educate for less, which the 2020 Global Pandemic has forced them to do. Some schools will figure it out, but others will not, and there likely will be a consolidation.

Tuition-driven schools recognize they can't charge lower prices and expect to stay in business for very long, which is why college administrations and faculty members must be frustrated with comprehensive remote learning or a hybrid model involving online and in-person classroom experiences. Even if the pandemic has proven to be a blip on the radar, two significant factors could force a pruning of the higher education landscape. One is that there are probably too many colleges in the United States to support the number of graduating seniors anyway. Another is that for at least the past 15 to 20 years, there has been a resurgence in educational training and apprenticeship experiences after high school, which in some instances will make students more willing to forego college.

Financial Aid Considerations

I raise these points because they provide a clearer understanding of how financial aid works. When joined together, need-based grants and merit scholarships essentially create financial aid. Depending on the school, students probably will receive of a combination of the two—both of which are free money that doesn't have to be repaid. Whereas need-based grants can go away if an individual's financial circumstance changes, merit scholarships have enduring value in that they generally won't change based on financial circumstance—making them the preferable part of the financial-aid equation. But as the name suggests, they come with an important string attached. In order to hold onto a $25,000 a year merit scholarship, most schools require students to rightfully maintain a 3.0 grade point average and some an even higher GPA. It's also worth noting that students need to reapply every year for need-based grants. Another part of the financial aid package may be a work-study line that's paid directly to students.

Students who rely on financial aid for college but also need to borrow money, typically a federal fixed-rate Stafford loan, will need to repay that debt. Mounting student loan debt has set back nearly 45 million borrowers about $1.56 trillion, averaging $32,731 per student and reaching crisis proportions across the United States.[20] It's not unusual for some students, particularly those who attend medical and law schools or pursue graduate work, to be saddled with six-figure debt after college. The situation is not lost on employers, a growing number of whom are offering student loan refinancing programs to save young workers thousands of dollars on interest payments. These programs have even eclipsed interest in 401(k) savings plans among new entrants into the U.S. workforce, serving as more of a tangible benefit. The notion of retirement can be far off for young folks who are barely making ends meet while paying off their student loans. President Joe Biden suggested a $10,000 forgiveness plan on the 2020 presidential campaign trail, which could generate an estimated more than $400 billion in aggregate savings, while some Democrats have advocated an amount that's as high as $50,000.[21]

Whatever the financial aid package ultimately looks like, it's always best for students to conduct a Net Price Calculator review on each college's website by entering their financial information before ever applying. Of course, more prestigious institutions are less likely to negotiate these packages than smaller, private liberal arts colleges. But the point is for students and their families to know up front exactly what they'll pay or will likely pay for higher education, especially at a time when more consumers expect transparent pricing of various goods and services. If financial aid is a consideration, what happens is students know the total cost of college when they apply, but generally they don't know what their financial aid will be until after that application is filled out and a decision is rendered. Students oftentimes receive an offer of admission first, and if everything was filled out completely and correctly, a financial aid offer would be received a few days later.

One noteworthy point is the complexity of using ED for committing to a university without having received a financial aid package. This is often why many families balk at ED, which is a misguided response. The fact is, nearly every school offers a Net Price Calculator on its website, providing relatively accurate idea of whether the family is need-based aid eligible and how much aid they may qualify for. If the calculation is wrong or a family's financial situation changes, there is a way out. Students who are unable to receive financial aid "may

Financial Aid Considerations

decline the offer of admission and be released from the early decision commitment," according to the National Association of College Admissions Counseling Statement of Principles of Good Practice, which governs all college admissions practices. Thus, financial considerations are not a good reason to forgo an ED application.

Earlier I addressed the idea of finding the right fit by matching a student's needs or desires to what colleges have to offer. The same is true when applying for financial aid. Let's say someone is accepted at five of the 12 schools they applied for and received a financial aid package from all of them. If they happen to pick five schools that are comparable to Rensselaer Polytechnic Institute (RPI) that are wrong for their income level, then they're stuck with five really poor financial options. However, if they had applied to Lehigh, which is ranked at the same level as RPI except for steep differences based on income level, then they might be in a great financial position.

Each school distributes financial aid differently. FAFSA requires that families fill out their expected contribution as part of the federal methodology, but there's also an institutional methodology that must be factored in to determine financial aid. That means the amount for state schools will differ from most private schools, depending on how that contribution is calculated. To help low-income and high-income families find the right financial fit for college, President Barak Obama required every school to include a Net Price Calculator on their website. I created five financial profiles for the families I work with: low-income, low-middle, middle, middle-high, and high—with a family of four ranging from $30,000 to more than $250,000.

What I have done is import these profiles into Net Price Calculators in the nation's top 50 schools and build an Excel spreadsheet for each of those categories. This strategy helps to determine which schools are distributing their aid in a way that is beneficial to families at each of those income levels. The results are striking. Schools that are ranked almost exactly the same would cost tens of thousands of dollars differently, especially over the course of four years. For example, I found that attending Swarthmore over Bryn Mawr was literally going to cost $60,000 more, even though they were ranked three and four in the country. I also learned that low-income students who applied to Lehigh received strong financial aid packages because their distribution strategy is focused on providing need-based aid to low-income families. RPI is the exact opposite. They distribute their aid quite widely to attract students from upper-income families.

What I always say to families is, it can feel like a backward process. When people buy a car, they don't drive it home and then learn how much it costs. But that's exactly how it is when applying to college unless the family makes use of the Net Price Calculator. Most families either don't know it exists or heard it's inaccurate (only when incorrect data in inputted), and therefore they don't want to use it. At any rate, for students who weren't born on third base and can benefit from the push for diversity or financial aid, there's another increasingly important component to consider when applying to colleges. Perhaps now more than ever, transfers from one school to another require a more thoughtful approach to leverage investment in higher education.

CHAPTER 10:
Thoughtful College Transfers

Many young people have no idea what career they want to pursue, much less focus on in their college studies, and in most cases there's no rush to figure it all out. This is why it's not at all unusual to come across undeclared majors. But deciding at least what to study is critically important for students who plan on transferring from one college or university to another. College majors are typically declared after the sophomore year—a process that differs from institution to institution, but the stakes are raised at highly selective schools if that decision comes later and must be accepted by the relevant department. For example, students who apply as a transfer for their junior year must often both pass the admissions committee review *and* departmental review. Students who apply as a rising sophomore will often only require an admissions review.

When I was at Cornell and thought, for instance, that a transferring freshman who's interested in computer science was pretty solid, then I could just accept his application without commiserating with others. If that same student applies as a sophomore, and I come to the same conclusion, then I'd have to send it to the computer-science department because he's now going to be declaring that major. The department might not share my enthusiasm because they're in a better position than me to judge his performance and potential, plus it's traditionally a highly competitive area. Complicating matters is that many kids enrolled at community college may decide to pursue an associate's degree and then transfer to a four-year school because once they get started, they may not want to part with new friends, a beloved teacher or other factors. While not impossible to transfer under these circumstances, it certainly isn't easy and must be factored into a student's college-transfer strategy. The bottom line is that generally it's best to transfer after freshman year.

One noteworthy trend that has been driving transfers in recent years is the rise of community colleges. They have come a long way with respect to not just preparing students for four-year degrees and career opportunities, but also partnering with four-year schools and industry. That's at least what I've experienced in most of my engagements with community colleges. They are incredibly connected these days. But it's easy to surmise why they're so appealing. Their average tuition and fees cost about one-third the lowest-tier public four-year university and one-tenth the lowest-tier four-year private university, according to the College Board reports.[22] Also, community college students who continue to live at home avoid room, board and other expenses, while in some states this type of education is free for first-time, full-time students. Community college students account for a small number of transfers, but many universities and even highly selective schools view their unique experience as adding a level of diversity—even if they're not individually diverse from an ethnic standpoint.

While community college is less expensive, I'd add an important caveat. Let's just say for argument's sake that a student applies to Lehigh and receives a $20,000 grant toward the $50,000 annual cost of tuition, then decides he can't afford the $30,000 tab. Plan B involves a community college that costs just $10,000, saving $20,000 on the aforementioned scenario. While he plans to transfer to a four-year college after his first year, it's important to realize that Lehigh's $20,000 grant might not still be there. That's because schools generally do not provide the same level of financial assistance to transfers as freshmen since they won't be there as long.

Now here's the rub: If the school doesn't have an articulation agreement, then the student probably should be applying to colleges that are relatively physically close to home. These agreements between the community college and university leadership, as well as faculties at both schools, guarantee that classes completed at a community college (or any school, for that matter) will count as credit toward a four-year university degree upon transfer. Oftentimes, these agreements require very in-depth conversations, especially in STEM areas. Since advanced calculus at a community college isn't the same as it would be at Cornell, for example, the conversations can be sticky. Once an articulation agreement is in place, it makes life so much easier for transferring students because there's a clear path for crediting courses that have been taken up to that point.

Another factor to examine is that the process of getting in as a transfer is easier because the applicant pool is significantly smaller than incoming freshmen from high school, thus the competition isn't as stiff. But in a year when the worst pandemic in a century turned higher education (and society) upside down, it will be interesting to see how it affects transfers at schools where higher learning is confined to comprehensive remote learning or a hybrid model that includes minimal classroom exposure. A larger consideration, of course, will be on decisions to invest in highly selective schools that keep students at arm's length and, therefore, vastly limit the potential of a truly unique and meaningful experience.

CHAPTER 11:
Impact of the 2020 Global Pandemic

Two chapters ago I referenced how the Great Recession and the 2020 Global Pandemic have been devastating to students and their families, but in my estimation the latter's impact will be significantly greater than the former. While the financial crisis squeezed ivory towers in terms of operating expenses, revenues and endowments and made higher education unaffordable for some, students weren't talking about it. The only relevant question was whether their parents had enough money to send them to college, and if the answer was yes, then life was still normal. The 2020 Global Pandemic, however, completely changed the game. It led to a startling drop in 2020 freshman enrollment at American colleges and universities of more than 16% compared to the previous year, according to the National Student Clearinghouse Research Center. Even enrollment at community colleges fell by nearly a quarter. NSCRC also found a 4% dip in overall undergraduate enrollment versus the fall of 2019. Interestingly enough, undergraduate enrollment fell in every region and type of institution across the United States. except four-year, for-profit colleges.[23] But it still doesn't change the fact that these developments foreshadow a wave of contraction and consolidation that will sweep over higher education in the years ahead.

The pandemic is affecting more than an ability to afford college tuition; it's actually changing the way colleges are able to evaluate applicants, which didn't happen in the Great Recession. Colleges still read applications the same way, but now many student bodies have been forced into a virtual learning environment. The trouble is admissions officers have no idea which districts have done a good job in the so-called new normal. I'm surprised to learn some amazing districts did a very poor job because they simply weren't prepared. Some fell woefully short of the mark, unprepared for meaningful interaction between students and teachers under the distance-learning model. Instead, these districts were caught flat-footed, with students basically watching YouTube videos and engaging in other static methods of learning as teachers and administrators struggled to use new technology. There were clear discrepancies between the educational experience of students during the pandemic in environments that weren't conducive to preparing for exams.

We also don't know the teacher perspective and one huge challenge was dispensing poor grades to students who were at home without access to the same level of resources, calling into question the integrity of 2020's transcript. A related concern is that AP exams were administered online as part of an open-book format, which has never been done before. How beneficial could that possibly be? Some of my students told me it was super helpful because they could look up answers to questions that stumped them and got them right. Others said there was no time to look up all the questions because they really needed to know all the material. So the online format didn't matter to them. AP exams are both a universal and objective indicator of student performance based on content. They don't involve teachers whose grading is subjective when factoring in that some will be easier on students while others will be harder. But because of some open-book experiences, along with flawed virtual environment, there were tests that didn't go through or got canceled like the SATs, which is another huge and unprecedented development that needs to be factored into the mix.

Since the response to the 2020 Global Pandemic was different from one state to the next, it left a patchwork trail not just based on the College Board, but on high schools that actually did the testing. So if a random high school in New Jersey wasn't comfortable testing because of the 2020 Global Pandemic, then kids in that area couldn't take the test. I have clients from New York driving to Connecticut and Maryland to take the SATs because they don't want to be part of the group that didn't get to take the test. The dynamic of review in the 2020 Global Pandemic environment is completely different than what happened in 2007, and I think it will spur long lasting changes.

Take, for example, SAT subject tests, which highly selective colleges seek to indicate a student's their relative strength in, say, physics or history. Yale decided very early on that not only was it not requiring SAT subject tests, but it wouldn't even review them. The reason is simple: School officials want the population of students who are not going to be able to do it to still apply. That's a whole different ballgame than pre-Global Pandemic. What's significant is the potential trickledown effect of that kind of decision from a place like Yale is rather significant. Once Yale weighed in, pretty much every highly selective school I am aware of followed suit about not wanting to see SAT subject tests. Although the entire Ivy League decided to go without SAT subject tests (as well as cancel winter sports and postpone spring sports), I'm guessing they are still going to do just fine. There's really no need for SAT subject tests anyway. It was like splitting hairs among these students and represents another barrier for underrepresented and low socioeconomic groups. Although there's an end in sight to the pandemic, the impact it has on college admissions will be long lasting as universities consider both financial viability and what information is necessary for admissions decisions. The fact is, however, that all such obstacles can be easily removed so that there's parity for students across all segments of society.

CHAPTER 12:
Achieving Parity in Education

There's an incredibly simple fix to the systemic problems of educational financing in the U.S., which is to equally distribute state-based funding for K-12 instruction across all public school districts. The problem is that our leaders haven't shown the political will or courage to make this change, and I'm blown away that we don't do it. Adopting this approach so would be transformative at a time of mounting interest in elevating the nation's social-justice movement—serving as a tangible reform that could make a positive difference. It also would provide more young students equal opportunities and a roadmap for lasting success. But until it actually happens, we will continue to see a fractured educational system whose patchwork of affluent and impoverished regions deepen the wedge between students born into privilege and poverty.

I have seen this play out in my home state of Pennsylvania's 500-plus school districts. On average the Keystone State spends a statewide median of $8,838 annually per student. For some comparison, Lower Merion School District in Montgomery County, PA spends the most on a per student basis at $17,409 per student and Mount Union Area School District in Huntingdon County, Pa. spends $6,324 per student. That means that Lower Merion spends 175% more per student per year than Mount Union. Over the course of the 12 years of education prior to college, Lower Merion will spend $133,020 more per student than Mount Union.[24] When one school is spending seven times the amount of another school, the school that's spending significantly less has figured out how to educate with fewer financial resources. It forces them to become more creative about how they educate students.

Children in poorly funded school districts don't have a chance. But if we had state-based funding that was distributed equally at the beginning of a young person's educational life, all students would have equal access to similar resources. Under the status quo, all of the best teachers eventually flock to districts that pay more, and if any work in a low-paying district, they just won't stay there for long. I believe that statewide school funding is absolutely necessary. Without this solution, we can expect more of the socioeconomic challenges that we see today. I'm not suggesting that equally distributing state funds for K-12 education would fix all of our problems, but it would at least even the playing field for young kids.

The benefits also would spill into higher education. One of the problems with college admissions is the crushing debt that many students are saddled with, even if they land well-paying jobs after graduation. With so many schools forced into online learning that's clearly not as strong as in-school experiences, it's a timely time to discuss the issue of educational parity. In some ways it took the massive upheaval of the 2020 Global Pandemic for educational administrators to begin to consider how to educate more efficiently. While there's some value in virtual learning, it doesn't replace the collegiality of face-to-face interaction and sense of community that develops when students learn together on a college campus. What we have seen is that schools can still deliver educational content at a significantly lower cost because there's less infrastructure. But for many years colleges have operated functionally with no interest in understanding how to educate for less. If anything, there has been a focus on what we can do with more resources as evidenced by ever rising tuition prices. But it appears there is some appetite for change as colleges consider how to manage a pandemic and unsustainable tuition trends.

To fully understand and appreciate the extent to which U.S. education is mired in inequality, a brief history lesson is in order. The current system's dependance on federal and state government sources to pay for college, as well as payments from students and their parents, surfaced after World War II. The reason many Americans attend state colleges is because most of the money was supposed to come from the state level. But states eventually realized that colleges would simply raise tuition if their higher-education budgets were cut. As such, the Center on Budget and Policy Priorities found that states slashed inflation-adjusted per-student spending 13% between 2008 and 2018.[25] While elite private and public schools are able to raise substantial revenue from tuition and alumni donations, most colleges struggle for resources—exacerbating inequality in higher education. The impact this has on many poor and middle-class students is unconscionable. For example, those who excel in high school and attend colleges with inadequate resources and low graduation rates run the risk of incurring debt with no degree and poor job prospects. Research suggests that college graduates are not only more likely to be employed and earn better salaries than those who didn't graduate, but also tend to be happy and live longer. Solving these problems will take tremendous effort, but some novel ideas have surfaced short of making all public colleges free to attend, which Bernie Sanders has endorsed and critics dismiss as wildly expensive. An education policy expert, for instance, proposed that colleges be given the option to receive more U.S. federal funding in exchange for charging a simple, affordable tuition.

Every single year, tuition prices continue to increase 2%, 3%, or 4% in virtually every school. That's because there's no cap on student federal loans (applicants may borrow "up to the cost of attendance"), which means most people don't end up paying out of pocket for college. Not many people can just write a $50,000 check, so instead they take out a loan. In some cases, students will pay off those loans, while in others the parents will pay them off. Nonetheless, it doesn't really matter. My point is that with students able to borrow as much money as they want, colleges can easily raise the cost of tuition the following year. The response is that students take out a little bit more loan money to get through college. In many cases, the difference between a $50,000 and $60,000 tuition bill that seems ridiculously high doesn't matter much to young students who are trying to earn a degree. All that matters in many families is that if their son or daughter are admitted to an elite school they might land a good job that will help them pay off that debt. That's generally the mindset I see from families, which is why they're willing to continue to pay these prices, and every year they go up a little bit more.

It's a vicious cycle that needs to be re-examined. But as long as parents are willing to continue paying inflated tuition bills and the government isn't limiting federal student loans, it will be difficult to assess the true value of an investment in higher education. In real estate, banks appraise the value of a home and impose limits on the money they lend to buyers. They don't give them *carte blanch* when lending money. There is no appraisal in education. The government just says, "charge whatever you want. We'll give you the money for it." And so schools have just been out there raising tuition, and quite honestly, there has been no impact to the institutions. But there's a prudent fix. I suggest capping U.S. federal student loans and re-examining the issue after five years or a decade. Colleges and universities would figure it out. They're teeming with smart people, administrators and faculty members with Ph.Ds. They would likely say, "Okay, we're not going to be able to increase tuition by 2%," and then determine how to educate students without that price hike.

Ultimately, the price we pay as a society for implementing these educational reforms will pale in comparison to the wasteful system that has long been in place. And it will be well worth the reinvestment in local communities. If states equally distribute educational funds to all of their school districts, basketball courts in wealthier areas may not be refinished every two years or there may not be an investment in other luxuries such as rock-climbing walls. The biggest sacrifice, of course, would be teacher salaries. There wouldn't have this mass exodus of teachers from poorer districts to richer ones if states evenly funded all of their school districts. In short, it would lead to an evening out of the teacher talent. Teachers who work in areas without enough financial resources routinely burn out after a few years and don't feel appreciated. Eventually, they seek employment in higher-income school districts to escape this cycle in search of stability, a pension and other benefits. Let's face it: not all teachers are created equally, and so the good ones generally move on if they're unhappy with their circumstances. With true educational parity in place, there would be a move away from almost the collegiate, country-club atmosphere that colleges have also started to build. And I don't believe students in affluent areas would lose out on anything that would fundamentally change their experience.

Of course, it's difficult to make such sacrifices when you're used to having your way, but I do believe if privileged people were truly educated about the obstacles underprivileged kids face, they would think differently about funding education. Most people have a soft spot in their hearts for children. If they walked into a public high school in inner-city Baltimore like I did and saw the environment that these students are expected to learn, grow and compete in, then they would be shocked. Any reasonable human being would say, "there's no way I could learn, grow and compete in that environment, so it's ridiculous to ask a 10-year-old to do so."

The type of changes I'm suggesting are evolutionary, but over time they can have a revolutionary impact. You can't just expect school districts to do this in one fell swoop, but I do believe that there needs to be a plan. Politics are all local, and so you would need a courageous state representative from your local district to say, "I'm running, and my plan is to take funding away from your kids." That's not a popular political statement and the candidate is unlikely to win. I think leaders need to both educate people about our obstacles and challenges, but also make tough decisions. To be clear, the impact of these difficult choices would be a better community for *all* of us. The greatest asset we have in our society is human capital. We would have nothing, if it wasn't for people doing meaningful things, and the more people we have ready, willing and able to contribute, the better it is for our society as a whole. At the state level, one can easily understand the challenges and obstacles of each region, and distribute their funds accordingly. I really don't think it's that hard and believe it could be done. The better educated we are as a country, the stronger we will be as a people and better to compete in an increasingly global economy.

AFTERWORD:
Remaining Objectively Reflective

I have been guided by some great professional mentors for whom I'm grateful and would like to acknowledge their impact on my work and life. It started with my parents who made me aware that nothing is impossible if we set our intention and put forth energy. My wonderful Italian mom dedicated her life to me, my brother and sister. One thing I will always remember about my mom was she tried to make learning fun. Whether it was a silly game or special snack, study time was engaging. Without her love, amazing food and unrelenting support, I certainly would not be where I am today. My dad, a Northampton County Court of Common Pleas judge and former elected district attorney for 28 years who tried 25 first degree murder cases, was like a superhero to me as a child. While he won re-election for District Attorney seven times, he also ran unsuccessfully as a Democrat for Attorney General of Pennsylvania and the U.S. Congress. One thing I will always remember about my father was his reaction to winning and losing. They were almost identical. Always gracious, always thankful. Each success or failure another step on the journey. Never too high, never too low.

Outside of my family, Leon Washington taught me an

invaluable lesson about objectivity and fairness when I worked for him at Lehigh University where he served as Vice Provost for Admissions and Financial Aid. I have since applied it to everything I do. For this reason, I have dedicated my book to him. Speaking with the cadence of a Baptist minister, I was always mesmerized by his words and wisdom. As I progressed through my career, Leon helped me recognize the importance of remaining *objectively reflective*, as he put it. After a long conversation in his office about a personnel issue, he stopped me in my tracks with a powerful analogy, suggesting that I grasp together my hands and closely observe them. He then asked, "Can you see your hands? Can you see the intertwined fingers?" I wondered where this was going before saying yes. "Okay," he answered. "Now bring those intertwined fingers close to your chest. Can you see them now?" Without hesitation, I answered no. "You need to make sure not to bring things too close, remain objectively reflective so you can see everything and then make your decisions," Leon explained. His words stuck with me. A very simple change in perspective can have a drastic impact in both good and bad ways.

Another former supervisor who left an indelible mark was Bernie Story, Vice President of Enrollment when I worked at Moravian College. More than 60% of what I learned about enrollment management—anything from ways to lower student admit rates to strategies to impact the quality of an incoming class—can be traced to him. Three other Moravian colleagues were also very influential. Erica Mondok, Director of Transfer Admissions, went above and beyond in that job—advising transferring students on what courses to take in a way that I found deeply inspiring. Jim Mackin, Director of Admissions, was a perfect middleman to negotiate reasonable goals that balance what an institution seeks with the energy and resources of the admissions staff. Angie Cologne, Assistant Director of Diversity Recruitment and my first *professional* friend, literally built a diversity recruitment program from the ground up, and I was fortunate enough to have a front row seat.

Two others I worked with at Lehigh helped shape my educational philosophy. Bruce Bunnick, Director of Admissions, helmed an open and fair selection process wherein admissions counselors' voices were heard and student interests were well represented. He wore a bowtie and is not only very impressively articulate but also down to earth and a dear friend. Krista Evans, with whom I shared a Senior Associate Director title, was my partner in crime. She was both coach and cheerleader, always pushing and coaching team members to grow.

Finally, I want to thank my amazing wife, Carolyn. Growing is accelerated (and more fun) for those fortunate enough to share the journey with a partner who provides unconditional love and support. Together, we look forward to helping our preschool daughter Addie become curious about learning and even grow her own ivy over time.

About the Author

John M. Morganelli Jr. has held several key positions in the college-admissions field prior to becoming one of the only independent admissions consultant in the United States who served as an undergraduate Ivy League Admissions Director. He was Assistant Dean and Director of Admissions for the College of Arts & Sciences at Cornell University, which is one of only eight Ivy League schools across the nation; Senior Associate Director of Admissions at Lehigh University, one of the top national research universities; and served in Assistant Director, Senior Assistant and Associate Director roles at Moravian College, America's sixth-oldest institution.

Morganelli earned a Bachelor of Arts at Villanova University and Master of Education at Lehigh University. Under his leadership at Cornell, the College of Arts & Sciences achieved its most statistically successful enrollment cycle ever for two consecutive years. While at Lehigh, he helped the school achieve both a lower admittance rate and higher SAT scores, a rare accomplishment in higher education.

Endnotes

1 Spradling, Jessica. "Origins of the Term 'Ivy League' Remain Mysterious." *The Badger Herald,* March 3, 2003. https://badgerherald.com/news/2003/03/03/origins-of-the-term/#:~:text=Some%20theorize%20that%20Ivy%20is,people%20actually%20used%2C%20Daniell%20said

2 Levenson, Eric. "Maryland CEO Paid Former Fencing Coach $1.5 Million in Bribes to Get his Sons Accepted to Harvard, Feds Say." *CNN,* November 16, 2020. https://www.cnn.com/2020/11/16/us/college-admissions-scam-harvard/index.html

3 "Timeline: The Major Developments in the College Admissions Scandal." *Axios,* August 21, 2020. https://www.axios.com/college-admission-scandal-operation-varsity-blues-51e66764-23b2-4539-ba05-d55740939c46.html

4 Woolfolk, John. "Stanford: College Admissions Scandal Mastermind Approached Seven Coaches." *Bay Area News Group,* December 3, 2019. https://www.mercurynews.com/2019/12/03/stanford-says-college-admissions-scandal-mastermind-approached-seven-coaches/

5 "Timeline: The Major Developments in the College Admissions Scandal." *Axios,* August 21, 2020. https://www.axios.com/college-admission-scandal-operation-varsity-blues-51e66764-23b2-4539-ba05-d55740939c46.html

6 National Center for Education Statistics. "Degree-Granting Postsecondary Institutions, by Control and Level of Institution: Selected Years, 1949–50 Through 2018–19." https://nces.ed.gov/programs/digest/d19/tables/dt19_317.10.asp?current=yes; "Number of Non-Degree-Granting Institutions Offering Postsecondary Education, by Control of Institution and State or Jurisdiction: Selected Years, 2000–01 Through 2017-18." https://nces.ed.gov/programs/digest/d18/tables/dt18_317.30.asp?current=yes

7 "Ivy League Tuition Comparison." *College Tuition Compare, 2019.* https://www.collegetuitioncompare.com/best-schools/ivy-league/

8 Parker, Tim. "What's an Ivy League Education Worth?" *NBC News,* August 29, 2011. http://www.nbcnews.com/id/44122857/ns/business-school_inc_/t/whats-ivy-league-education-worth/

9 "Cooper Board Approves Plan to Return to Full-Tuition Scholarships." *The Cooper Union,* March 15, 2018. https://cooper.edu/about/trustees/board-approves-fec-plan

10 Korn. Melissa. "Acceptance Rates at Harvard, Other Ivy League Schools Edge Up." *The Wall Street Journal,* March 27, 2020.

11 Caster, Andrew. "What are the Benefits of an Ivy League Education?" *AllPeers.com,* March 18, 2020. https://www.allpeers.com/what-are-the-benefits-of-an-ivy-league-education/https://features.thecrimson.com/2018/freshman-survey/makeup/; https://features.thecrimson.com/2018/freshman-survey/makeup/

12 Bolluyt, Jess. "These Are the Presidents Who Attended Harvard and Other Ivy League Schools (and How Donald Trump Compares)." Cheat Sheet, January 14, 2019. https://www.cheatsheet.com/culture/presidents-who-attended-ivy-league-schools.html/

13 "Should I Choose an Ivy League School?" *Affordable Colleges Online,* November 10, 2020. https://www.affordablecollegesonline.org/college-resource-center/considering-ivy-league-education/

14 Cornell University/Typical SAT scores. 2018–2019. https://www.google.com/search?q=Cornell+average+SAT+score&rlz=1C1AVNE_enUS687US688&oq=Cornell+average+SAT+score&aqs=chrome..69i57.329j0j15&sourceid=chrome&ie=UTF-8

15 The Common App. 2020. https://www.commonapp.org/about

16 Biskupic, Joan. "Affirmative Action: Challenge to Harvard's Admissions Practices Hits Federal Appeals Court." *CNN,* September 16, 2020. https://www.cnn.com/2020/09/16/politics/affirmative-action-harvard/index.html

17 "Department of Justice sues Yale, alleging race-based discrimination." Associated Press, October 8, 2020. https://www.cbsnews.com/news/yale-university-sued-by-justice-department-alleging-race-based-discrimination-2020-10-08/

18 Caldera, Camille G. "Legacy, Athlete, and Donor Preferences Disproportionately Benefit White Applicants, per Analysis." *Harvard Crimson,* October 23, 2019. https://www.thecrimson.com/article/2019/10/23/nber-admissions-data/

19 Burstein, Ellen M. "Harvard Endowment Returns 7.3 Percent for Fiscal Year 2020." *Harvard Crimson,* September 29, 2020. https://www.thecrimson.com/article/2020/9/29/harvard-endowment-fy2020/#:~:text=Harvard%20Management%20Company%20returned%207.3,largest%20sum%20in%20its%20history

20 Friedman, Zack. "Student Loan Debt Statistics In 2020: A Record $1.6 Trillion." *Forbes,* February 3, 2020. https://www.forbes.com/sites/zackfriedman/2020/02/03/student-loan-debt-statistics/#51cc6505281f

21 Cox, Jeff. "Biden's Plan to Forgive Student Debt Could have Limited Economic Benefits, and Carry Risks." *CNBC,* December 6, 2020. https://www.cnbc.com/2020/12/06/bidens-plan-to-forgive-student-debt-could-have-limited-economic-benefits-and-carry-risks.html

22 West, Charlotte. "With Higher Ed in Limbo, Students are Switching to Community Colleges." *NBC News,* May 20, 2020. https://www.nbcnews.com/news/education/higher-ed-limbo-students-are-switching-community-colleges-n1210656

23 Hubler, Shawn. "Freshman Enrollment has Dropped More Than 16% from Last Year at American Colleges and Universities — and by Nearly a Quarter at Community Colleges." *The New York Times,* October 15, 2020. https://www.nytimes.com/2020/10/15/world/freshman-enrollment-drops-significantly-at-us-universities-and-community-colleges.html#:~:text=Freshman%20enrollment%20has%20dropped%20more,Clearinghouse%20Research%20Center%20reported%20Thursday

24 Murphy, Jan. "PA. School Districts that Spend the Most (and the Least) to Educate Kids." PennLive, May 22, 2019. https://www.pennlive.com/news/2018/02/school_districts_that_spend_the_most_and_the_least.html

25 Mitchell, Michael, Michael Leachmann and Matt Saenz. "State Higher Education Funding Cuts Have Pushed Costs to Students, Worsened Inequality." *Center on Budget and Policy Priorities,* October 24, 2019. https://www.cbpp.org/research/state-budget-and-tax/state-higher-education-funding-cuts-have-pushed-costs-to-students

www.ingramcontent.com/pod-product-compliance
Lightning Source LLC
Chambersburg PA
CBHW060847050426
42453CB00008B/881